Boom!
Zap!
Pow!

TEACHING ONOMATOPOEIA

BY LISA OWINGS

Published by The Child's World®
1980 Lookout Drive • Mankato, MN 56003-1705
800-599-READ • www.childsworld.com

ACKNOWLEDGMENTS
The Child's World®: Mary Swensen, Publishing Director
Red Line Editorial: Editorial direction and production
The Design Lab: Design

Photographs ©: Red Line Editorial, cover, 1, 2; Piotr Krzeslak/
Shutterstock Images, 4–5; Shutterstock Images, 6, 8, 9, 10, 12,
15; Kiselev Andrey Valerevich/Shutterstock Images, 6–7; Phil
McDonald/Shutterstock Images, 11

ISBN 9781503808324
LCCN 2015958426

Printed in the United States of America
Mankato, MN
June, 2016
PA02304

ABOUT THE AUTHOR

Lisa Owings has a degree in English and
creative writing from the University of
Minnesota. She has written and edited a wide
variety of educational books for young people.
Lisa lives in Andover, Minnesota.

Onomatopoeia is the use of words that imitate sounds. Look for **onomatopoeia** in this book. You will find it in **bold** type.

Kara heard rain on the roof. **Boom**! Thunder sounded.
Lightning **zapped** a power line. The lights went out.

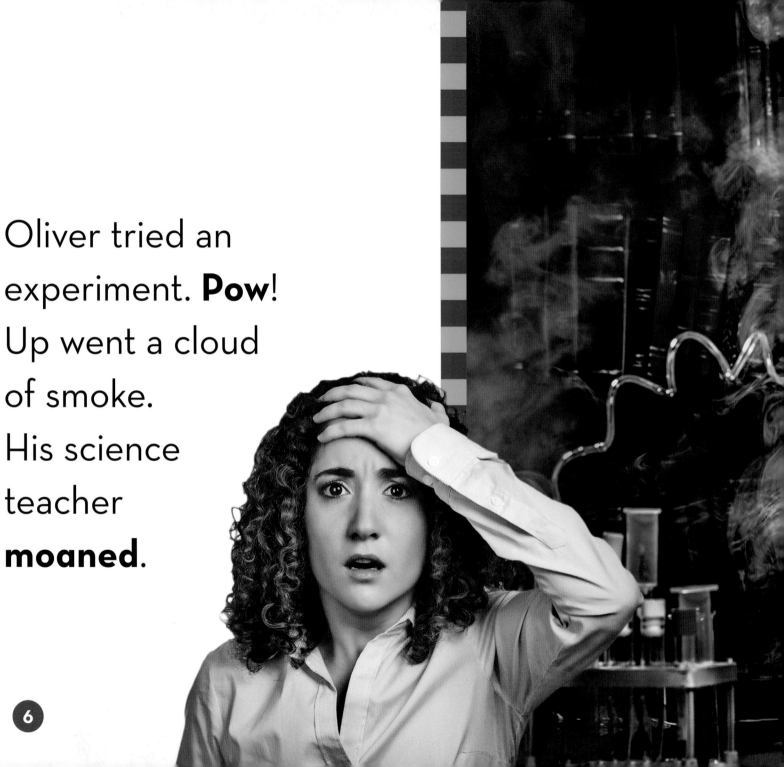

Oliver tried an experiment. **Pow**! Up went a cloud of smoke. His science teacher **moaned**.

Simon jumped into the pond with a **splash**.
Croak. He was face to face with a frog!

Bacon **sizzled** in the pan. Malia was hungry.
The egg fell on the floor. **Splat**!

Snow **crunched** under Toby's boots. The wind **howled**. Toby **zipped** up his coat.

Hiccups kept Lisa awake.
She got up and **gulped** down
some water.
Then she **flopped** onto her bed.

Did you hear onomatopoeia?

boom	moaned
croak	pow
crunched	sizzled
flopped	splash
gulped	splat
hiccups	zapped
howled	zipped

To Learn More

IN THE LIBRARY
Judge, Lita. *Red Sled*. New York: Atheneum Books for Young Readers, 2011.

Marsalis, Wynton. *Squeak, Rumble, Whomp! Whomp! Whomp! A Sonic Adventure*. Somerville, MA: Candlewick, 2012.

Sutton, Sally. *Demolition*. Somerville, MA: Candlewick, 2012.

ON THE WEB
Visit our Web site for links about onomatopoeia: **childsworld.com/links**

Note to Parents, Teachers, and Librarians: We routinely verify our Web links to make sure they are safe and active sites. So encourage your readers to check them out!